A Trip Through the
United States

by Anika Brennan

SCHOOL PUBLISHERS

Cover, ©age fotostock/SuperStock; p.3, p.8, p.12, ©PhotoDisc; p.5, ©Creatas Images/PunchStock; p.6, ©James J. Stachecki/Animals Animals; p.7, p.11, Courtesy NPS; p.10, ©Corbis; p.13, ©Corel; p.14, ©Corbis/PunchStock.

Cartography, p.4, p.9, Joe LeMonnier

Printed in China

ISBN 10: 0-15-350249-5
ISBN 13: 978-0-15-350249-1

Ordering Options
ISBN 10: 0-15-349939-7 (Grade 4 ELL Collection)
ISBN 13: 978-0-15-349939-5 (Grade 4 ELL Collection)
ISBN 10: 0-15-357300-7 (package of 5)
ISBN 13: 978-0-15-357300-2 (package of 5)

1 2 3 4 5 6 7 8 9 10 985 12 11 10 09 08 07 06

420
H 257
Gr. 4
Suppl.
Curr.

The United States is a huge country. The land reaches from the Atlantic Ocean to the Pacific Ocean. There are many different kinds of land in the United States. There are wide-open spaces and forests. There are tall, beautiful mountains topped with snow. There are many wonderful sights to see on a journey across the United States.

Regions of the United States

The United States is divided into five regions. The name of each region tells where it is found. The regions are the Northeast, the Southeast, the Midwest, the West, and the Southwest. These regions are shown on this map. Let's take a trip through each region in the United States. We will begin our journey in the Northeast.

The Northeast

The Northeast includes the states of Maine, Vermont, New Hampshire, Massachusetts, Rhode Island, Connecticut, New Jersey, Pennsylvania, and New York. Many northeastern states lie along the Atlantic Ocean.

As our tour takes us into the state of New York, we pass the Adirondack Mountains. The Adirondacks are separated from the Appalachian Mountains by Lake Champlain on one side and the Mohawk River on the other. The Appalachian Mountains stretch all the way to the southern part of the United States.

Adirondack Mountains

The Southeast

In many areas of the Southeast, there are areas that are wet for most of the year. These places are called wetlands. Many wetlands are found along the coastline, where the land meets the ocean.

If we go all the way south to Florida, there is a huge wetland called the Everglades. Many interesting animals are found in the Everglades. Alligators and crocodiles are two of the many kinds of animals that live in the Everglades.

Great Smoky Mountains

As we move up along the west coast of Florida, we look out over a sea called the Gulf of Mexico. Soon we travel north through the states of Georgia and Alabama.

Now we reach another southeastern state called Tennessee. Here, we find the Great Smoky Mountain National Park. The Great Smoky Mountains stretch from North Carolina into Tennessee. The Smoky Mountains are covered in thick forests. Some of the mountains are very tall.

Now we travel alongside the largest river in the United States, the Mississippi River. The river begins in Minnesota and runs all the way south to Louisiana. There, the mouth of the river flows into the Gulf of Mexico. The Mississippi River is more than 2,300 miles (3,701 km) long. As we ride along the river, we pass through flat, open spaces. Patches of land are dotted with farms and fields filled with wheat, corn, and tall grasses.

The Midwest

Our trip takes us north through the states of the Midwest. Some of these states are Ohio, Indiana, and Michigan. Here we come to five very large lakes. These are called the Great Lakes. The Great Lakes are shown on the map on this page. The largest is Lake Superior. In fact, this lake is the largest freshwater lake in the whole world! Boats travel across the Great Lakes. They carry goods from one state to another. People go boating and swimming in the Great Lakes, too.

Rocky Mountains

The West

Next, we travel to the states of the West. First, we see lots of flat land. This area is called the Great Plains. Then, we notice some mountains in the distance. They are the Rocky Mountains. These mountains make up the largest mountain range in the United States. They reach all the way from Mexico to Canada. Some peaks in the Rockies are so tall that they are covered with snow all year.

The West is not only made up of mountains. In some states like Utah and Nevada, there are wide-open spaces called deserts.

Deserts are lands that get very little rain. Cactus plants grow well in the desert. Cactus plants have sharp spines on them. We see tall columns of rock as we travel through the deserts of Utah. There are also mountains with flat tops on them.

Then we come to a huge lake in Utah. This lake is called the Great Salt Lake. It is the largest saltwater lake in the United States.

Death Valley

Now we are traveling west. Here we come to the states that lie along the Pacific Ocean. These states are Washington, Oregon, and California. In the north, Oregon and Washington are states that are covered in forests with tall evergreen trees.

Farther south, California has forests, but it also has desert land. An area called Death Valley is the hottest place in America! Now we travel through the Sierra Nevada Valley to the states of the Southwest.

The Southwest

The states of the Southwest are Arizona, New Mexico, Texas, and Oklahoma. All of these states, except Oklahoma, lie along the border of Mexico.

The Southwest has deserts, too. The Colorado River cuts through the desert lands of Arizona. For millions of years this river has flowed. It has carved out a huge, deep canyon called the Grand Canyon. A canyon is the space between two mountains. As we pass by the canyon, you can see the colorful bands of its rock walls. The Grand Canyon is one of the wonders of the world. It is more than 270 miles (434 km) long!

Then we come to Texas, the last stop on our journey. Texas is the second largest state in the United States. The only state larger is Alaska, which is far to the northwest. Parts of Alaska are covered with frozen land called the tundra. Our fiftieth state, Hawaii, is made up of islands in the Pacific Ocean. Hawaii is far southwest of the rest of the United States. Hawaii is filled with beautiful flowers and high mountains.

Each state in the United States has its own landforms, rivers, plants, and animals. That is what makes all of the states so special!

Hawaii

Scaffolded Language Development

VERB CONJUGATION Model for students how to conjugate verbs using the verb *to travel: I travel, you travel, he/she travels, we travel, they travel.* Have students repeat the conjugation with you three times. Then have students chorally read each sentence below, and say the sentence again using *you, they,* and *she* as the subject.

1. I take a train out West.
2. I fly on a plane to Denver.
3. I raft down river rapids.
4. I go to Nevada.
5. I plan on going again next year.

 ## Science

Make a Booklet Help students find vocabulary words in the book that describe the different features of land in the United States, such as deserts, lakes, and mountains. Then make a booklet of these words. Ask students to write definitions and draw pictures to illustrate the words.

School-Home Connection

Your State Ask students to talk with family members about your state. Are there mountains, deserts, plains, or rivers in the state?

Word Count: 974 (1,018)